Robbing

GOD

Then He spoke many things to them in parables saying: "Behold, a sower went out to sow. And as he sowed, some seed fell by the wayside; and the birds came and devoured them.
Some fell on stony places, where they did not have much earth; and they immediately sprang up because they had no depth of earth.
But when the sun was up they were scorched, and because they had no root they withered away.
And some fell among thorns, and the thorns sprang up and choked them.
But others fell on good ground and yielded a crop: some a hundredfold, some sixty, some thirty.
He who has ears to hear, let him hear!"

Matthew 13:3-9
NKJV

Robbing GOD

RANDALL M. MOONEY

Crossover
PUBLICATIONS

Robbing God

BY: RANDALL M. MOONEY

Copyright © 2009 by Randall M. Mooney
All rights reserved.

This book or parts thereof may not be reproduced in any form, stored in a retrieval system, or transmitted in any form by any means – electronic, mechanical, photocopy, recording, or otherwise – without prior written permission of the publisher, except as provided by United States of America copyright law.

Published by Crossover Publications LLC, 870 N. Bierdeman Road, Pearl, Mississippi 39208, www.crossoverpublications.com
(601) 664-6717, Fax: (601) 664-6818

Scripture quotations noted KJV, from The KING JAMES VERSION of the Bible.

Scripture quotations noted CEV, from the CONTEMPORARY ENGLISH VERSION, Copyright © 1995 by The American Bible Society, New York, NY. Used by permission.

Scripture quotations noted NKJV, from THE NEW KING JAMES VERSION, Copyright © 1979, 1980, 1982, Thomas Nelson, Inc., Publishers.

The Bible text designated NASU is from THE NEW AMERICAN STANDARD BIBLE UPDATE. Copyright © 1960, 1962, 1963, 1968, 1971, 1972, 1973, 1975, 1977, 1995, by The Lockman Foundation. Used by permission. All rights reserved.

Scripture quotations noted NASB, from the NEW AMERICAN STANDARD BIBLE ®, © Copyright The Lockman Foundation 1960, 1962, 1963, 1968, 1971, 1972, 1973, 1975, 1977. Used by permission.

Scripture quotations noted NLT, from the HOLY BIBLE: NEW LIVING TRANSLATION, Copyright © 1996. Used by permission of Tyndale House Publishers, Inc., Wheaton, Illinois 60189. All rights reserved.

Library of Congress Control Number: 2009907826
ISBN 978-0-9819657-1-0
Printed in the USA

Cover design by: R. Matthew Mooney
Cover concept and background artwork by: Randall M. Mooney

DEDICATED TO:

THE LORD JESUS—HE GAVE IT ALL FOR THE JOY THAT WAS SET BEFORE HIM, AND I CHEERFULLY FOLLOW, GIVING IN HIS FOOTSTEPS!

Table of Contents

1   Introduction to the Parable & the Conflict

9   Chapter 1: Part 1 of the Parable,
                         "Payday"

17   Chapter 2: Part 1 of the Conflict,
                         "The Good Investor"

27   Chapter 3: Part 2 of the Parable,
                         "Saturday Morning"

35   Chapter 4: Part 2 of the Conflict,
                         "Prosperity Preaching"

41   Chapter 5: Part 3 of the Conflict,
                         "Someone to Blame"

47   Chapter 6: Part 3 of the Parable,
                         "Afternoon Emergency"

51   Chapter 7: Part 4 of the Conflict,
                         "The Root of Evil"

61   Chapter 8: Part 4 of the Parable,
                         "Stressing Sunday"

67   Chapter 9: Part 5 of the Parable,
                         "The Sunday Offering"

83   The Summation

89   Chronology of Scriptures

Introduction to:

The Parable
&
The Conflict

What happens to the *spirit of generosity* of the average person when the economies of the world melt down around them? How will charitable individuals, that have been committed *givers,* navigate through budget breakers like runaway gas prices, high food costs, unemployment, and tax increases to pay for a government spending frenzy?

Furthermore, with all the talk of Jesus' imminent return—what if Jesus does not return in the Christians' lifetime, and their retirement plans vanish along with the hopes of Wall Street?

Robbing God is simply a book about personal freedom—a freedom that is experienced when individuals discover the kind of giving first demonstrated by a loving God. God did not withhold anything from those he loved, and he proved that love with the delivery of his own son on a cross. Somehow, as with many of the Bible's teachings and principles, some have managed to turn the act of giving into little more than a self-serving, personal agenda complete with greed and corruption. While some may teach that giving produces personal gain and wealth, many give for the sheer joy and privilege of being the giver rather than a receiver. God was the ultimate giver, and he created us in his image. We can certainly be at our best when we learn to give cheerfully, just as he gave.

The parabolical portion of our story begins on a Friday afternoon, when a *typical family* collects their paycheck for the week, and concludes in church on Sunday morning when presented with the traditional morning offering. The story attempts to capture some of the emotional situations that confront the average family trying to cope with the needs of their household. Some of these families may find themselves hit from different angles by religious broadcasters, or other televised religious programs, using Bible verses to make promises and guarantees of personal wealth—all for the price of a few dollars.

Unfortunately, some among those *persuasions* use cunning and deceitful practices to get *typical families* to give up some of their hard-earned money through hype, deceit, manipulation, and guilt. Some even stoop so low as to intimidate uninformed people into giving to them by suggesting they are guilty of *robbing God* if they fail to send money to their *so-called* ministries. The *robbing God* technique has become a popular method used by some to keep those cards and letters flowing into their mailboxes—especially if those letters contain checks and cash.

Throughout the chapters of this book, I have separated the story of our family and what they are dealing with from the other chapters that offer some historical and biblical explanations for this current mindset. I also offer observations and some fresh insight into how some in the Christian culture have reduced cheerful giving into another form of religious bondage, emotional torment, and even personal resentment for a few—often brought on by guilt-driven manipulation. In addition to the biblical and religious reasons for giving, some families are torn between the choice of feeding their families, paying their bills, or planning for their futures, while facing the pressures of being over taxed, over spent, and solicited on every hand to give to a myriad of causes.

The conflict intensifies as folks wrestle with their sense of loyalty to themselves and the needs of their local church. What comes first...the offering plate or the dinner plate? With the economy in turmoil, pressures have mounted on the family, forcing them to opt for their basic need over what they have believed was their spiritual and Godly duty. Many churches and charitable organizations that depend on the generosity of simple wage earners for their existence are also feeling the crisis.

The book also points out that givers and receivers alike equally share some of the distortions about giving. Greed, covetousness, and the fleshly desire to get something for nothing continue to enable *inexperienced farm hands*, if you please, to send their seed to another man's field. They then have the nerve to sit back and expect a great harvest in their own field, where they have planted nothing. Then they erroneously blame God for failing to keep his promise to them when there is nothing growing in their field—again, a field in which they planted nothing.

While the subject matter of this book visits some of the Old Testament's treatment of tithing and the New Testament's instructions to give cheerfully, the intent of the story is not to besmirch or discourage giving. It is, however, intended to encourage giving for the right reasons, and in a more fruitful and enjoyable manner. By Sunday morning the parabolic family and their local pastor discover a wonderful reality about giving without the fear, guilt, or coercion often associated with *free-will* offerings.

People should not treat charitable giving as bill paying. Giving can and should be a cheerful expression of love and generosity that results in tremendous joy, satisfaction, and encouragement for those who learn to skillfully participate in a gift of love. When the family and the pastor in our parable discover the real meaning of cheerful giving, they find themselves blessed with more in life than just money.

During the years from 1999 through 2008, I drove an average of over one hundred thousand miles per year across the southeastern United States. The construction company I operated had a working relationship with a restaurant chain headquartered in Texas. We oversaw the building of over forty restaurants for that company in ten states from Texas to North Carolina. During that time on the road, I spent an average of five nights a week living and working out of a motel room.

In every new town, I found myself reviewing the yellow pages in local phone books and monitoring the local television channels to get a feel for the spiritual temperature of that given area. The yellow pages revealed the number of churches in the area and their denominational affiliation. The cable channels aired a variety of religious broadcasting in a given area. The area of interest and of most concern in each community was the type of programming that obtained financial support from the local population. Most Christian programming depends on support by contributions from viewers in a local area. It was interesting to learn what local Christians were willing to pay for on their local airwaves.

In many instances, various religious television programs used unbiblical and manipulative methods to raise financial support. Most of that support came from average working people with average incomes, trying to make ends meet. The most common use of terminology involved the words "make a seed faith offering" and suggested great financial gain for giving, along with the occasional warning not to be guilty of "robbing God" for not giving. I believe that type of coercion has no other motivation than to make money through generating fear and guilt rather than encouraging generous and cheerful giving.

Some of those television ministries went to great lengths to promise *hundredfold blessings* in return for sowing seed faith financial gifts into their ministry. They would also parade people across the screen, with testimonies of having received large, unexpected sums of money only days after sowing seed faith offerings into those ministries. The stunning part of my observation was that many of the Christians I discussed those issues with were afraid to question or say anything negative about the practices used by some ministries to solicit money. Some even believed them wholeheartedly, and had themselves sent money to some of those television ministries. Please don't misinterpret my motivations—I'm perfectly fine with people giving their money to anyone they choose; it is the root cause of their motivation that causes me concern.

I also noticed some similar characteristics in people who were *givers* and people who were *gamblers*. Among the states that offered lotteries and the states that allowed casinos, a "money-for-nothing" mindset was the key to the success and prosperity of the casinos and the state lotteries. The "money-for-nothing" mentality also appeared to be somewhat characteristically similar for some of the people who responded to the pleas of "seed faith/robbing God" television programs. All of the giving and the gambling promised the possibility of substantial returns on a minimal investment. In each of those scenarios, one could possibly have been a gambler at heart to participate. I also concluded that if the love of money was the root of all evil then all of us, whether in church, in a casino, or in the lottery ticket line might need to grind some stumps in our own back yards.

With this book, I attempt to demonstrate parabolically some examples of how many givers give for the wrong reasons and motivations. Therefore, they miss the real joy of giving. It is also sad to note that many have simply given according to the way they were taught, and that for the benefit of someone other than themselves and their own families. When I first set out to write this book, I thought to approach it as a theological study—my initial goal being to instigate discussion and debate over the methods used by some people to raise money. I had grown tired of hearing news reports about televangelists and their multi-million dollar houses, their jet planes, and their many fine cars. I was equally worn out with *so-called* reality shows about casinos and poker marathons.

The *real* reality show aired when Jesus transformed the world and history without any of those opulent luxuries or excesses. I have contended repeatedly in my communications to people that the *American Dream* and the *Gospel of the Kingdom of God* are not compatible. Contrary to the views of some popular preachers and their teachings, the gospel has never been a lottery ticket for creating overnight millionaires. Many wealthy people in the world do not espouse a belief in Jesus Christ, nor in his mission on earth. There have even been examples of some Christians who were guilty of attempting to avoid productive work in the hopes of growing wealthy by throwing money at empty promises in exchange for sudden and unexpected prosperity.

Instead of trying to write yet another expositive book on the subject, I decided to write a *parable* included with a mild attempt to explain it in clear and simple terms. Jesus often spoke to people in parables—then later, he would explain the parables to his disciples privately. I also determined the story needed to be to the point, and that it should allow the reader room to come alongside the characters in the book. In addition, it should encourage as well as educate. Still, if no one gets the point, then it fails to enlighten and encourage freedom in the area of our giving. I also firmly believe that some of the issues dealt with in this book are *roots* that hinder spiritual growth—and that an axe needs to be laid to those roots of greed and evil in order to guide us into a more desirable and even profitable place of giving to God, and to each other. If the *love* of money is in fact the root of all evil, then there is much evil that needs to be rooted out of our hearts by laying an axe to the root of the money tree within our own lives, and possibly in our own churches.

Chapter One:

Part 1 of the Parable

"Payday"

Friday Mom always got off work earlier in the afternoon than she did on the other days of the week. She started work at 5:30 a.m., instead of the usual 8:00 a.m., so she could leave early. Dad, however, usually was stuck at the office a little later on Fridays, so he took care of getting the kids off to school on those days. He also dropped the baby off at the sitter's house on his way to the office.

Mom tried so hard to get out of her office promptly at 2:30 p.m., but someone always wanted to stop her and talk about something that usually could wait—or at the very least could have easily been answered by one of the other staff. Nevertheless, Mom was never rude regardless of being a little impatient. She would always stop and listen, pretending not to be in that big of a hurry, despite the fact that she actually was in a hurry. Today was no different—making it to the door, and almost escaping, she met one of the club members at the exit door, and of course, they just had to talk to Mom. Mom just stood there, purse in hand and backpack on her shoulder, holding the door half open, listening, smiling, and hoping her audience of one would notice her anticipation to finish her exit. They didn't notice, and she continued to patiently listen. Eventually, they said all they had to say, and Mom politely said goodbye as she continued her rush to the car.

Mom's first stop was the bank, where she waited in the line at the drive-through to cash her check. The wait was not as long for her because she beat the afternoon payday rush on the bank. Her next stop was the baby sitter. She picked up the baby, paid the sitter, thereby experiencing the first demand on her paycheck of the day. With baby in tow, she then stopped at the local grocery store to get a few of the things they had run out of during the week. Mom and Dad would go for their big shopping day on Saturday, when they had time to make a list and stick to their fragile budget. Mom hurried through the grocery store as quickly as she could while having to wrestle with a fidgety baby. The store was full of other mothers doing the same thing she was—the checkout line was frustrating. She had to hurry because she still needed to get the other children from the neighbor's house where the kids went to stay after school.

Dad finally finished his last task for the day and rushed away from the office to get to the bank before they closed. Paydays were the days he wished he could bring himself to trust direct deposit instead of having to rush to the bank before they closed at six. In the car, Dad turned on the radio to get a jump on the news of the day before getting home. Mom didn't care for the news, and Dad tried not to wear her out with the 24-hour news channels going all evening. He was concerned about today's financial news, because of some of the things he had overheard other employees discussing.

While sitting in the long line at the bank's drive-through, and hoping the tellers were fast enough to get to him before the six o'clock close, Dad listened carefully as the newscaster of his favorite channel talked about the stock market falling that week with the biggest crash since The Great Depression. The news was unsettling to say the least. All the talk of market failure, bank collapses, home foreclosures, and bankruptcies of some of the nation's largest and most prominent companies had a way of draining Dad's peace of mind. He knew the fine line his family walked with their budget, and he understood there was little room for any surprises. He was already upset that it had cost him over one hundred dollars the last time he filled up his SUV with gas.

Meanwhile, Mom, still trying to get over the cost of a gallon of milk wrestled with the baby, her purse, a backpack, and two bags of groceries. Half the time she felt like a pack mule trying to get into the house. First, she changed the baby's diaper, and then she walked next door to pay the neighbor for watching the rest of her children after school during the week. Mom and Dad willingly paid the neighbor for her service in order to prevent their children from being latchkey kids. Admittedly, though, they couldn't wait until their oldest child was old enough to baby sit so they could save some money. Their oldest child, however, wasn't in a hurry for that time to come.

Back at the bank, dad finally got to the window and cashed his check. The teller looked at him and asked how he was doing. Dad, responding to the things he had been hearing on the news (more than responding to her request), returned the greeting by asking the teller how she was doing and if the bank was okay. The young teller reported that all was well, but Dad believed her face was telling a different story. They concluded their exchange; she sent Dad's cash through the sliding drawer, and she wished him a nice weekend. Dad said nothing more and moved forward as an impatient driver behind him tapped his horn.

As Dad drove away, he turned the radio back up so he could hear the chatter about the weeks market blow up. Dad didn't pretend to be much of an investor, and his retirement plan wasn't enough to get excited about, but he was concerned about the way the economy might affect his job. He knows that he would be in trouble if either he or his wife were to be laid off from their jobs.

Dad left the bank and headed up the road to their favorite pizza parlor. Dad bought pizza for dinner and headed to the house. Neither he nor Mom felt up to cooking on Friday nights, and the kids were way too hungry to wait, so pizza always seemed to be the best solution. Besides, the kids were still excited about pizza Friday. Mom and Dad had turned this quick, inexpensive dinner into a Friday night tradition, although they had long since lost their enthusiasm for the pie.

Dad finally made it to the house. All the kids acted as if they were starving and rushed Dad in the driveway, knowing that he had pizza on-board. Dad, kids, and pizza quickly made it into the house. There would be no formalities; the den was the dining room tonight, with paper plates, plastic cups, and pizza in front of the television.

Dad, of course, commandeered the remote control. Dad had a unique skill. He could eat a slice of pizza with one hand, hold his drink-filled plastic cup between his legs, rest his paper plate on top of the cup, and still flip channels with the other hand. Dad first turned to the news channel. It was filled with talk of collapse and government bailout. After getting *that* look from Mom that clearly instructed him to change the channel, he immediately complied and moved on to something else. With every passing channel, somebody in the room would yell for him to stop because they saw something they wanted to watch. Even so, Dad remained undaunted in his quest to know what was on every channel before settling in on the one show he might be interested in watching—or the one that drew the least number of complaints.

Mom was tired and the baby was fussy, so she could have cared less what was on TV. The kids finished their pizza and lost interest in the TV altogether...and in the so-called *family time*. The kids headed off to different parts of the house after dinner to find alternative entertainment, something more to their liking.

Later that evening, Mom got the kids in bed and Dad carried the pizza boxes and the rest of the trash out to the trash bin. Dad then grabbed the mail out of the mailbox, mail that had gone undisturbed until now. While thumbing through the stack, he separated the junk mail, the advertising flyers, the magazines, and the bills. He then carried them all into the house and tossed them on the desk in the den to deal with later. Exhausted and beyond frustration, Mom and Dad finally sat down in the den to recover from their week of work, including their evening of work at home. Mom relaxed by reading a book, and Dad continued to find solace in channel surfing.

Mom and Dad did not have as much of a religious nature as some people they knew, but they had tried to live their lives in a way that they believed was pleasing to God. They had been faithful to each other in their marriage. They had carefully nurtured their children by teaching them about the love of God, the Golden Rule, and the Ten Commandments. They had attended Sunday school and church services as regularly as they could with their busy schedules, and they tried to be generous givers of their time and money. In fact, if they had the means to do so, they would be extravagant givers, because they really were loving and unselfish people.

Nevertheless, they have lived with a dirty little secret—a secret they have always felt guilty about and one that they found very difficult to discuss with their pastor. This couple had struggled with the guilt and shame of not being able to afford to tithe regularly at the church they attended. They always had the greatest of intentions when they worked on their budget, but somehow the money always disappeared much faster than could be imagined.

No matter how much money they made, the demands of maintaining a home, children, and transportation only left them feeling like guilty failures before God when the offering plate passed in front of them at church. They still gave. But they struggled with giving ten percent from a budget that sometimes demanded one hundred and ten percent of their income. Sometimes they gave twenty percent. Other times they gave three percent. Most of the time they gave out of guilt and self-induced pressure, because they had been taught to believe that anything less than ten percent amounted to robbing God.

Furthermore, if Dad didn't have enough guilt about his financial failures at church, channel surfing added its share of bad economic news mixed with television preachers piling it on with images and appeals to send money to help every cause and desire they felt God wanted them to address. Often, every petition to send money included a promise of great blessing and reward to the givers. Some even contained a reminder of the curses to come if the summons went ignored. Dad quickly moved on to the next mindless sitcom in order to avoid the seeming condemnation, and Mom sat quietly reading her book.

Chapter Two:

Part 1 of the Conflict

"The Good Investor"

There are many historical explanations as to how we got to this point regarding giving. In the pages to follow, it is my intent to bring freedom to the human heart and to rid us of the condemnation that has been perpetrated upon us in the area of giving. I plan to do this in simple and plain terms in order to deliver anyone, from the simplest of thinkers to the most educated, from the snare of giving out of guilt, fear, and coercion. In the process, we will discover how to live and give joyfully, and how to acquire the ability to recognize the many ways to be a cheerful giver, loved by Almighty God.

Just as our Creator has always loved to give good things to his children, he imparted to his loved ones the desire to help and give to others. Our very nature compels us to use our talents and resources to be helpful to other people. If we are in a room full of family and friends watching a young baby pull up on various things in the room, we will all assist at the first inclination of the baby's need for help. If the child shows any sign of falling as he attempts to take steps away from an object he or she is relying on for support, simultaneously every witness in the room will reach out to help. We cannot help but do that.

It is rare for any of us to see children, the elderly, or the poor in need without feeling some sort of pity, compassion, and a desire to help. Unfortunately, we have also seen our emotions preyed upon by the unscrupulous actions of different individuals. Their selfish behavior has left many of us cynical when confronted with what appears to be real needs. Nevertheless, most of us will give, and those of us who do give appreciate the satisfaction which giving to others gives to us.

In the twenty-fifth chapter of the book of Matthew, Jesus was sitting on the Mount of Olives speaking privately with some of his disciples. He shared with them information about the end of the age and told them several different parables. Many times Jesus spoke to the multitudes in parables. Later he would often explain the parables to his disciples when he could get alone with them. The following parable actually provides tremendous insight into the act of giving. Please read it carefully.

Again, the Kingdom of Heaven can be illustrated by the story of a man going on a long trip. He called together his servants and entrusted his money to them while he was gone. He gave five bags of silver to one, two bags of silver to another and one bag of silver to the last—dividing it in proportion to their abilities. He then left on his trip.

The servant who received the five bags of silver began to invest the money and earned five more. The servant with two bags of silver also went to work and earned two more. But the servant who received the one bag of silver dug a hole in the ground and hid the master's money.

After a long time their master returned from his trip and called them to give an account of how they had used his money. The servant to whom he had entrusted the five bags of silver came forward with five more and said, "Master, you gave me five bags of silver to invest, and I have earned five more."

The master was full of praise. "Well done, my good and faithful servant. You have been faithful in handling this small amount, so now I will give you many more responsibilities. Let's celebrate together!"

The servant who had received the two bags of silver came forward and said, "Master, you gave me two bags of silver to invest, and I have earned two more."

The master said, "Well done, my good and faithful servant. You have been faithful in handling this small amount, so now I will give you many more responsibilities. Let's celebrate together!"

Then the servant with the one bag of silver came and said, "Master, I knew you were a harsh man, harvesting crops you didn't plant and gathering crops you didn't cultivate. I was afraid I would lose your money, so I hid it in the earth. Look, here is your money back."

But the master replied, "You wicked and lazy servant! If you knew I harvested crops I didn't plant and gathered crops I didn't cultivate, why didn't you deposit my money in the bank? At least I could have gotten some interest on it."

Then he ordered, "Take the money from this servant, and give it to the one with the ten bags of silver. To those who use well what they are given, even more will be given, and they will have an abundance. But from those who do nothing, even what little they have will be taken *away. Now throw this useless servant into outer darkness, where there will be weeping and gnashing of teeth." (1)*

The most significant difference in the treatment of the three servants was the amount of silver that each one received. The master, an investor, knowing his servants' capabilities, gave each one of them an amount to invest that contributed to their success. The master had not favored one over the other; he had simply made provision for each of them to succeed at the task set before them. He did not try to trick them. He simply wanted them to reach their greatest potential.

When the master later returned, he gathered the three together to see how they had done. The first two did exactly as he had hoped they would. They had invested the master's money wisely and verified their success by doubling his money. However, when he questioned the third servant, all he got was an excuse and an accusation.

The third servant told the master that he knew he was a hard man to work for. He also accused him of reaping where he had not planted. What was wrong with the third servant's accusation? The servant had failed to recognize that his master had entrusted and invested in him with his time and money. The servant was insinuating that the master had done nothing for him. Furthermore, he also failed to take ownership of the investment money. Due to his fear of being a failure, he took the money and buried it so as not to chance losing the money. At one point he even told the master, "Here is your money back."

This angered the master, partly because there was no truth to the accusation that he reaped where he had not sown, and because he knew that the principle of sowing and reaping was a beneficial and legitimate means of growing assets. He had successfully reaped by exercising this principle, and had enjoyed its fruitfulness by investing in others. In addition, the servant deprived the master of any celebration he could have enjoyed because of the servant's success. Instead, the servant feared the master, because he misjudged the master's heart towards him. So he buried the money in the earth for fear of losing it.

Then the master went further to expose the lazy servant's hypocrisy by telling him that if he really believed he was such a hard man, the least he could have done was place the money in the bank to earn interest. As a result, the master cast this lazy, fearful, and unprofitable servant into the outer darkness.

Interestingly, the master had not asked for his money back from any of the three servants, despite the lazy servant offering to give the money back. The master took the unprofitable servant's money and gave it to the servant that had been the most profitable. The master had plenty of money. It was not about the money—it was about investment in the three servants. His desire was for them to grow and become successful with the gifts he had given them. The lazy servant would have failed with one talent or one hundred talents, because of his attitude towards the master and himself.

Here are a few thoughts to consider about ourselves: (1) we are made from the dust of the earth; (2) we have all been given certain talents and abilities from our creator; and (3) the easiest way to recognize those talents is to consider what comes easiest for us—what we are the most passionate about doing. When we ignore or fail to recognize our talents and abilities for whatever reasons, we are in essence burying them inside of us (the earth) because of our fear of failing.

Consider the beginning, when God created everything. He spoke the worlds and the stars into existence with his word. However, he formed man with his own hands using the elements of the earth he had created with his word. He carefully and wonderfully fashioned our bodies from the resources of his own creation. He worked with his hands and personally invested in our formation.

Furthermore, he imparted the same creative talent in each of us to work with the resources of his creation in order to extend and increase his investment and his kingdom. We are able to take something as simple as sand and make bricks, blocks, and even glass to build beautiful buildings in which to live and work. We take trees and fashion them into lumber to build our houses, our furniture, and a multitude of other things.

Man is continually relying on the resources and the elements of God's creation to make cars and fuel, buildings, electronics, and aircraft, in order to realize the greatest fulfillment and potential of God's investment in each of us. This investment in us has grown greater than all the generations before us, and will no doubt continue to grow.

We dare not accuse God of being a hard man, as the servant did of his master, and declare that God has done nothing for us. We must not believe as that lazy servant did that he has given us nothing to invest for growing our lives and his kingdom. If we believe that God is that hard to serve and please, then we could quite possibly meet the same fate as that lazy and unprofitable servant. On the one side, we see a servant delivering accusations to his master for being a hard man who receives fruit despite putting forth little or no effort. Then we see the benefit of being faithful and wise investors with the resources freely provided to us. It is entirely up to us as to what we will reap. Certainly, it can only be what we have sown.

What can we conclude about the accusation? Is there anyone on whom this type of incrimination could justly fall? Yes! Throughout history, we have seen examples of dictators, world leaders, politicians, and even religious leaders using deception, manipulation, and outright lies to enrich themselves from the fruit of hardworking people everywhere. Greedy men have manipulated financial reports solely to garner profits, and to influence markets while risking the money of others for their own personal gain. These shysters have used everything from force to false theology to reap the fruit of the seeds sowed by the unsuspecting contributors. The *Good Master* is not one of those unscrupulous practitioners.

A dictator uses the force of an army to overthrow a government for the *so-called* good of the people, only to line his pockets with the blood and the money of the very people he is claiming to help. In a less deadly, but no less brutal fashion, *Mom's* and *Dad's* have been instructed by people claiming to be men and women of God to send their tithes and offerings so they can share in the reward of souls being won to the kingdom of God.

As with dictators, crooked politicians, and greedy executives, we have also seen our share of religious men proclaiming their mission statements in hopes of inspiring people to send in *seed faith offerings*, promising abundant prosperity to the givers. Still, there are far too many stories which have come to the surface of opulent lifestyles, million dollar homes, fine cars, outrageous shopping sprees, and multi-million dollar jets that have been purchased with the money given by the faithful and adequately fleeced givers, yet those doing the receiving have only appeared to give to themselves.

I believe shame belongs, in many instances, to the givers *and* the receivers. We should be ashamed for giving to this form of debauchery for no other reason than our own greed for personal gain. Those abusing the gifts of God, and the gifts of the givers, should also be ashamed, and surely they will face accountability. It does not take a lot of money, television airtime, expensive cars, or jet planes to share the good news of the kingdom of God with your friends and neighbors. From the time of Christ's earthly ministry to the present, the gospel message has always found its greatest expansion because of faithful believers sharing the good news with others. We can do more good with a cool glass of water and an encouraging word than all the television preachers combined.

The master gave the servants the supplies, instructions, and the encouragement to make wise investments. Two of the three demonstrated to themselves and to the master that his investment in them was a wise decision; it was in fact, a very profitable decision. The lazy and fearful servant only complained and accused the master of being a hard man for whom to work.

Our giving should always be a joyful and generous investment in the gifts that God has placed in us. That does not mean we cannot be successful. That does not imply that we cannot celebrate a profit. What it does show is that we reap what we plant. If we work hard and sow many seeds, we will have a huge harvest. If we plant little, we will reap little as well.

Chapter Three:

Part 2 of the Parable
"Saturday Morning"

It was Saturday morning, and Mom and Dad were busy cooking breakfast for the hungry family. For whatever reason (no one is ever sure), the children were always a lot more awake and rowdy on Saturday mornings. Mom and Dad would love to sleep in, but the kids always made sure that didn't happen. During the week, when everybody had to be up for work and school, they could barely dynamite the kids out of their beds. Today, they were up with the sun.

After breakfast, Dad cleaned the kitchen, and Mom got started on a week's worth of dirty laundry. Willing or not, the weekend ritual started with a kamikaze approach to a myriad of chores and duties that everyone but the new baby got to help with. The kids were all sent to their rooms and throughout the rest of the house to search for dirty laundry, as if the load already in the laundry room wasn't big enough. Mom trailed behind the kids picking up the socks they dropped along the way. Dad finished the dishes, wiped the stove and the counters, and headed for the vacuum cleaner. Dad was actually proud of how domesticated he had become. Mom was always bragging on him to her friends, and their husbands would call Dad telling him he kept them in trouble over all the housework they heard about. Dad always remembered their complaints and had a big laugh when he was doing housework. He grinned sheepishly to himself, knowing he was piling it on for his less than domesticated friends.

Dad started the vacuuming. The younger children wanted to ride, but Dad let them wrap around his legs instead. He tried to make the chores into a game to alleviate the sheer misery of the task. Mom kept her focus on the laundry. She didn't want Dad's help, because his idea of doing laundry involved tossing everything in together without separating things. She thought he probably did it on purpose to avoid what he considered an undesirable chore. Nevertheless, Dad would put the clothes away for Mom after everything was finished. Mom admitted Dad was the better organizer and packer of the two.

After the floors, Dad moved out to the yard, which was in great need of some attention. He was good at that chore, and the older kids were still young enough for him to make a game out of getting them to help. He could get it done faster working alone, but he enjoyed the time with his kids. They liked taking turns riding the lawn mower with Dad. Weed eating was no fun, but they had a blast with the leaf blower. A stray football in the yard also provided a good distraction from the yard work.

By noon most of the work was finished, and everybody was starving. There always seemed to be one last load of clothes in the dryer. Mom was already feeding the baby when Dad and the other children came in from outside. Dad prepared sandwiches and punch for the kids, and Mom took a shot at folding the last load of clothes while the kids kept the baby entertained in the high chair. Eventually Dad headed for his favorite chair in the den with a couple of sandwiches and a glass of milk. He, as usual, had to ask if anyone had seen the remote control for the TV, and as usual, he found it stuffed under the cushion where he was sitting. He sat there eating, drinking, channel surfing, and recouping from the morning's chores. He glanced over at the desk in the den with a week's worth of unopened bills waiting for his attention, and he got a tinge of heartburn. He started the mental process of tackling the bills while finishing his glass of milk and looking for a football game.

While looking for a game, he noticed that nearly every channel had someone buzzing about the economy. Dad thought his economy hadn't been good for a while, and he hated to think what his world would be like if things really got bad. He knew it helped to keep his mind on God, and that it was best to trust him during tough times. Finances were often the first attack the enemy used to steal Dad's peace of mind.

Meanwhile, Mom was in the kitchen cleaning up after the family lunch and began looking through the refrigerator and the pantry to make a list for the weekly outing to the grocery store. The children were growing like weeds, and along with their growing appetites, she had noticed a marked increase in the price of food and the amount of money needed to shop each week. She had particularly noticed a dramatic rise in the prices of things she most often needed. She knew the family had to eat, so she contemplated ways to cut back on other items in their budget in order to maintain balance. Mom and Dad made a decent amount of money together, but they had to watch what they spent very closely, because it didn't take much to blow the budget and rattle their world.

Dad finished his lunch and slipped off into a nap in front of a football game that failed to keep his interest. He snored through the sound of the TV and the yelling of the kids as they ran through the den letting the doors slam behind them. Mom put the baby down for a nap and took some time for herself before the trip to the grocery store.

The kids still couldn't make up their minds if they wanted to be in or out.

When Dad awoke from his nap, he made his way over to the desk and started looking through the mail. There was nothing worth looking at in the junk pile, so he tossed it all in the trash. Then he added the magazines to the stack of future reading material. He started opening the bills by their order of importance, and began entering them into his planner by their due date. Then he tried to determine what would have to be covered with this week's money, ran the numbers, and tried to figure out what was left for food, gas, and the usual surprises. There are always surprises!

Suddenly, Dad looked at his budget with a tinge of frustration as he realized that he hadn't figured in their ten percent tithe. The pastor always insisted that they give on Sunday morning in order to discover the route to true financial prosperity, but with the news channels screaming "recession" in the background, prosperity was not what Dad was feeling. He then started over with his calculations, and this time took ten percent off the top of the family's joint income for the week. He deducted the cost of the pizza, the neighbor's help with the kids, the baby sitter, and then looked again at the items that had to be paid this week. About that time, Mom handed him the grocery list with her estimate of how much it would cost to feed the family before their next pay period, and what extra she might need for the mid-week trip to restock diapers, milk, and bread—and Dad unraveled.

Next, Dad's frustration morphed into a low-grade anger, an elevated resentment, fear, and plain old guilt. That ten percent was really going to take a toll on the budget this week. He tried hard to space out the due dates for the mortgage payment and the car notes so they wouldn't be so hard to deal with in conjunction with the utilities, the insurance, and the credit card bills. Nevertheless, some weeks were tougher than others, and this was one of those weeks!

Dad got angry with himself, and a little at God, because he felt it was just too difficult to make it with the financial needs of his family on the money that they made. Even his recent raise had little effect, because the family needs continued to outpace the family income. He often struggled with resentment, because it didn't appear to him that his friends were struggling as hard as he did just to get by every day. He also had issues with the preacher, because he saw him living in a house paid for by the church, and driving a car given to him by one of the rich people in the congregation. The new building fund and every other fund the board voted to proceed with had turned the morning worship service into a weekly fund raiser and had reduced the amount of preaching time to lend more time to the appeal for more money to pay for all of those projects.

Meanwhile, Dad knew people in the congregation who couldn't pay their light bill, yet they got turned down for help from the benevolence committee because they made too much money. None of that felt right to him. Furthermore, he couldn't turn on the TV without having to deal with financial doomsday prophets, infomercials, and TV preachers, constantly begging viewers to buy something, or send *seed faith money* so all their financial worries would *miraculously* disappear. Then there was the guilt that he had to deal with. He knew that contentment with godliness was great gain. He even taught his children not to covet the things the other kids in the neighborhood possessed. God had blessed him and his wife with great jobs, and they were making better money than they ever had. But, life was hard in today's economy and they never seemed to have enough. Dad even hated to hear other people grumble and poor mouth. He despised it even more when *he* complained. He loved to give, and last week he had paid another young couple's light bill after the benevolence committee had turned them down. He often felt the committee's reasoning for rejecting requests for help was insensitive and unfair.

Most of all, he felt guilty because he would give the shirt off of his own back to help anyone, but he had been pounded on about tithes and offerings to the point that it felt like another bill to him rather than an opportunity to give generously. He had grown to hate his struggle between feeding the family, paying his bills, and feeling guilt-tripped to give God his portion. Church used to be encouraging for him. Now he felt like he had to deal with God's collection agency over past due bills. He got enough of that at home on the phone. Sometimes he just felt ashamed.

Mom interrupted his mental warfare and informed him it was time to go shopping. Dad threw the pencil on the desk and grabbed the checkbook; they loaded the kids into the van and headed off to the local grocery store. Dad knew he would have to return to the budget battle later because for now they had a family to feed.

Chapter Four:

Part 2 of the Conflict

"Prosperity Preaching"

About five hundred years ago there lived a man who was as frustrated with the financial mentality of the church of his day as Dad was in our little story. His name was Martin Luther, and history showed us that he was quite put-out with a common practice that the church used to raise money. Now granted, the church was one of the few places in his day where you could go for hospital care and charity.

But, sending proctors throughout the community to beg for money to keep those ministries going had proven to be most unsuccessful. Regardless of how good and noble the ministry of caring for the sick and helping the poor may have been, it was the constant begging for money by the proctors to keep those ministries going that wore the people of that day out.

Therefore, someone invented the concept of purgatory and the selling of indulgences. Those concepts were heavily practiced throughout Europe by the late thirteenth century, and as amazing as it was, they became very lucrative for the Catholic Church for years to follow. Once someone realized the proctors had failed at getting the people to give charitably to the Church's noble causes, some priests became skilled at selling worthless certificates known as indulgences to people who were willing to buy themselves and their relatives out of purgatory.

This may have been the Church's first model of what today has become known as the *prosperity doctrine*. When Europe made the transition from a barter culture to a mercantile society, and money became the more common method of exchange, the Catholic Church became quite skilled at making money for their notable causes by selling people the assurance they needed for eternity.

Martin Luther, having been educated in the Bible and its teachings, despised the fact that priests were using the practice of selling indulgences to the people as a means to receive God's mercy and grace. It was his understanding that the gift of God had been provided free to all mankind.

He also understood that God's only son, Jesus, had purchased that special gift with his life. Therefore, Luther began to publicly challenge this manipulation of the truth of God's grace. He opposed the selling of redemption and offering the value of good works for money.

Contrary to commonly accepted thought, Luther had not originally intended to leave the Catholic Church over this issue. He simply wanted the Church to repeal the unbiblical practice and return to preaching a gospel that depended on the finished work of Christ rather than the bartered works of men. His determination to get the church off of their detour of using that deceptive practice eventually got him thrown out of the priesthood which he loved and was committed to. However, history also shows that Luther's message resonated throughout the world for centuries after his death. Despite his being rejected by his fellow ministers, to this day we still enjoy the fruit of the stance for biblical truth that Martin Luther took.

Today, we have once again found that some leaders in various areas of influence have devised their own method of *selling indulgences.* Knowing better than to offer an eternal reward for the right price, some have resorted to offering a promise of prosperity and abundant living before reaching eternity's entry door. They insist it can be accomplished, according to their teachings, by sending a *seed faith offering* to their ministries. To drive the point even deeper, they offer testimonials of people who report receiving large and unexpected sums of money after following their instructions. In every case, they offer Bible verses and a guarantee that it works for anyone who believes and sends them a check.

However, it is nothing more than manipulation and coercion to solicit money. Although it is not practiced by every ministry, we can still see evidence of various forms of this practice from some of the smallest of churches to the largest of television endeavors. There is no doubt that it costs money to operate a business. However, is it really a faith-based operation when every marketing trick known to man is employed to keep it going?

The primary issue is that the practice deviates from the simplicity of the gospel message. Contrary to contemporary religious perception, the gospel can accomplish its intended purpose without the need to conform to the tactics and the production methods of the world. In fact, throughout history persecution did more to grow the church than glitz and glamour. Men and women willing to give themselves for the cause of Christ continue to convince a hostile world that the gospel will not be stamped out with force.

Nevertheless, some within the church's own ranks have done a better job of quenching the passion of their message by conforming to the world and incorporating the world's practices. Oddly, even a world in darkness can see through the deception of those espousing light for money. The reality remains that the *"American Dream"* and the *"Gospel of the Kingdom of Christ"* are not compatible.

The Apostle Paul declared in Romans 1:16,

For I am not ashamed of the gospel of Christ, for it is the power of God to salvation for everyone who believes. (2)

It was Paul's unashamed and open declaration of the gospel, and his reliance on the power of the gospel, that allowed him to be one of the most successful handlers of the message of Christ. Paul was a preacher who had no problem working with his own hands and doing whatever he had to do in order to not become a burden to the churches in which he worked. He was not willing to make the gospel message ineffective by using deceitful and manipulative practices. He declared himself to be a servant and even a slave to the cause of Christ, and he lived by the message he preached.

Furthermore, Paul wasn't some backwoods, ignorant man. He came from status and education. He knew what it was to be respected and preferred among men. He chose to be a man without respect and reputation for the cause of Christ. As a result of Paul's choice to be a servant, rather than to be served, we can still read about his life and be encouraged by his message two thousand years later. Paul, more than Hollywood, projected a more excellent method to proclaim and demonstrate the power of God through his powerful message.

Chapter Five:

Part 3 of the Conflict

"Someone to Blame"

Not all of the blame for our present weakness of spirituality can be placed at the feet of a few certain preachers. Their *gospel of gain* would be ineffective and could not be successful were it not for the thousands of individuals sending them millions of dollars. Just as the selling of indulgences worked because the church of that century had buyers, the prosperity gimmick works because of individual greed and the love of money. Granted, for some it might be plain, simple need and desperation.

We are inundated with offers of *something for nothing* at every turn of our television's channels. Lotteries and casinos have become deeply entrenched in many states and countries. People appear to show little reluctance to giving their hard-earned money to these business enterprises. In some cases, entire life savings and retirement funds have been relinquished on the hope of *striking it rich*. Despite how good a person might be, the love of money and the greed for riches entices them to spend a few dollars on the remote chance of winning millions. The companies that operate the casinos know the odds are in their favor. That is why they build such elaborate facilities and luxurious complexes, designed to lure us and our money into their establishments.

Apparently, their enticements are working, because we see people buying lottery tickets and visiting gambling halls in record numbers. Our state governments want us to feel good about bringing our cash to their causes by promising they are using the money for children's education and the welfare of the elderly. The casinos, on the other hand, have stockholders to answer to and are quite open about making a profit. All of this works because people are willing to put out a little, hoping to win a fortune.

As Christians, we tend to think we are smarter than the rest of the world and far nobler in our causes. However, some preachers and religious establishments are banking on the same principles as the casinos and the lotteries. Their message may sound different and more spiritual, and we may feel more justified in our giving, however, the principle is the same.

They present us with biblical authorization, promises, and substantiation to sow our seed or send our money to them so God can bless us and reward our tribute one hundred fold. So we send the money and wait for God's blessing. We buy the lottery ticket and pray to be the winner. We drop our money in the slot, pull the lever, and wait to hear the bells announcing our new fortunes. What's the real difference? We gamble to win, and most of the time, we lose. However, if we give to God and don't appear to win, we blame him like the servant who accused his master of doing nothing for him.

Gambling is not sowing. Reaping is not winning something for nothing. The farmer understands this principle more than all of us. He does not give his seed to someone else to plant in their field. He knows that the only way to reap a harvest is to work in his fields, sowing his seed and trusting that his hard work will result in a bountiful harvest. When that harvest comes in, he can sell the fruit of his labor, and he can freely give a portion of his increase to those less fortunate. He can even give seed to someone else to do as he is doing, but he must retain his *starter seed* for the next season of sowing.

When we are confronted with the offer to give up our seed for someone else to sow for us, we should resist their promise of easy money and do our own work. That was the problem with the third servant. The master said he was lazy and cast him into darkness.

We *should* be givers, but our giving needs to be cheerfully offered from the increase of our hard work. We should not give as the result of emotional manipulation or out of lust for easy riches.

> *Remember this—a farmer who plants only a few seeds will get a small crop. But the one who plants generously will get a generous crop. You must each decide in your heart how much to give. And don't give reluctantly or in response to pressure for God loves a person who gives cheerfully.*
>
> *And God will generously provide all you need. Then you will always have everything you need and plenty left over to share with others. As the Scriptures say, "They share freely and give generously to the poor. Their good deeds will be remembered forever."*
>
> *For God is the one who provides seed for the farmer and then bread to eat. In the same way, he will provide and increase your resources and then produce a great harvest of generosity in you. Yes, you will be enriched in every way so that you can always be generous. And when we take your gifts to those who need them, they will thank God.*

So two good things will result from this ministry of giving—the needs of the believers in Jerusalem will be met, and they will joyfully express their thanks to God. As a result of your ministry, they will give glory to God. For your generosity to them and to all believers will prove that you are obedient to the Good News of Christ.

And they will pray for you with deep affection because of the overflowing grace God has given to you. Thank God for this gift too wonderful for words! (3)

Chapter Six:

Part 3 of the Parable

"Afternoon Emergency"

The family van pulled into the driveway, the doors slid open, and the children attempted a getaway, only to be stopped by Dad. There were a lot of bags to carry in, and everyone needed to help. Even Mom, with the baby, a diaper bag, and her purse, managed to snag a couple of the smaller plastic bags. One by one, the family and the groceries all ended up in the kitchen.

Mom changed the baby and put him in the playpen so she could help in the kitchen. The rest of the kids were digging through the grocery bags looking for the newly purchased snacks, and Dad was trying to put everything away. Mom let him do the packing and restocking, because he always got the stuff neatly put in its place. Mom joined the rest of the family in the kitchen when the whirlwind of activity was at its highest point, and helped Dad survive the kids' snack attack and the remainder of the restocking.

Things calmed down as the kids went outside to play. Mom put the baby in the playpen and grabbed her book, hoping to get in a few chapters before starting dinner. Dad took the grocery receipt, sat down at his desk to make entries into the check book, and revisited the bill folder. At first glance, he was happy that the mortgage wasn't due that week. The utilities, cable bill, and the van payment needed to come out of this week's money.

Again, Dad checked the due dates, the amounts due, the bank balance, and then felt the need to check his blood pressure. It sure took a lot to live these days, and it didn't appear that their salaries were going to keep up with their expenses. The groceries and the high price of gas for the cars had been real budget busters. Dad thought it was all a conspiracy to keep gas prices high. They had spent a little more money at the grocery store than they should have, but they needed some things they didn't normally have to buy every week. The van payment was a must, the utilities couldn't wait, but he could stretch the cable bill another week before they threatened to disconnect it. He didn't want to run short of money in the upcoming week.

Dad made out the checks and paid the bills he decided would get paid that week. After he got everything ready to go in Monday's mail, he organized his desk and relocated to his favorite chair. Sitting with the TV remote in hand, he spent a few irritating minutes listening to the gloomy financial news, and then decided he was not in the mood for finances or politics. Since he couldn't find a worthwhile football game, he settled for an old movie and soon fell asleep in his easy chair for a short-lived nap.

Suddenly the back door slammed shut and Mom screamed! Dad jumped straight up out of his chair from a dead sleep. Quickly regaining his faculties, he discovered the source of all the commotion. One of the children appeared to have been hit in the mouth with something—a baseball, and was doing some serious bleeding from a split lip. Dad quickly assessed the situation and realized this wouldn't get fixed with a band-aid. He put a towel over the child's mouth and told Mom (he knew she couldn't handle this) to hold the towel over his mouth and don't look at it. Mom looked anyway and immediately started crying. The oldest child grabbed the baby, Mom held the towel, and Dad rushed everyone back into the van and away they went to the after-hours clinic for, hopefully, nothing more than a few stitches.

A couple of hours later, the family headed home, hungry, unnerved, and relieved that a few stitches did the trick. Nevertheless, cooking dinner was out of the question, and a drive-through bucket of chicken was what everyone agreed to. The clinic wanted payment immediately. They preferred that Dad file his insurance and wait for reimbursement—and Dad's budget was shattered. Dad loved his children and would do anything for them, but he hated surprises when he worked so hard to maintain a financial balance for the household. He had good insurance at work, so he knew he'd get the money back. Even so, he needed his cash this week.

 Later that evening when the kids were in bed, Mom and Dad talked about their day and about one of the only topics that could strain their relationship—their money.

Chapter Seven:

Part 4 of the Conflict

"The Root of Evil"

For the love of money is the root of all evil. (4)

Money is not evil. The first thing we need to lose is the guilt and the shame of having or not having money. It is obvious that we no longer live in a barter economy. It takes money to function in this world. That money comes in different forms—cash, debit transactions, credit cards, and checks. These are just some of the exchange methods which, once again, have changed the many ways people view and deal with money. Some are no longer comfortable with cash. Debit cards are growing in popularity. In some economies, cash is even avoided because of all the requirements necessary to deposit or explain large sums. Regardless of our feelings about money, none of us enjoys not having any.

The Mom and Dad in our story are clearly hard working people. They struggle sometimes to function on the amount of money they possess. They like spending a little of their money to do the things they enjoy, and sometimes they will spend on things they could have done without. But they don't live with an obsessive desire to be rich, nor do they try to live beyond their means. They love each other. They love their children. And their motivations for their family's needs are rooted in love, not greed. Because of their love, money simply serves as a tool to do the things they love to do, for the ones they love.

As previously stated, the love of money is the root of all kinds of evil. Some have scoffed at this verse and declared that it was the lack of money that was truly the root of all evil, but these are the same people who fail to recognize that money in and of itself has no value. That is the real reason money works in a mercantile based financial system. Unlike the barter system, where the value of items traded and the need or desire for the traded items determines the value of the deal, money, having no barter value of its own, can be exchanged for more desirable goods. Simply put, Mom is given money for her work, and she uses the money she is given to trade for the baby sitter's services and to buy food from the grocer. This way, she doesn't have to trade her personal possessions or handmade crafts for the things she lacks or needs, or can't produce for herself. However, without money being the method of exchange, she would have to find someone who was willing to trade her for the items she needed.

Most of the world no longer needs to trade a chicken for a gallon of milk. Money has enabled us to live in societal settings where *trade* relies on the skills and commerce of the individuals within that society. Everyone working within that system has the means to acquire the things they each need. The fact that money allows a society to function demonstrates that the money is not the evil.

Evil takes place in the hearts of the individuals within the social structure. Therefore, the love of money (not necessarily the use of money) becomes the root that evil hearts use to practice evil acts upon others within the social environment. Money does not commit evil, but evil men filled with wicked desires have committed all kinds of crimes against their fellow man because of, and for the love of, money. A cure for this can be found in the Bible. God's words not only show us how to live; they show us how to live with others.

> *When you follow the desires of your sinful nature, the results are very clear: sexual immorality, impurity, lustful pleasures, idolatry,*

sorcery, hostility, quarreling, jealousy, outbursts of anger, selfish ambition, dissension, division, envy, drunkenness, wild parties, and other sins like these. Let me tell you again, as I have before, that anyone living that sort of life will not inherit the Kingdom of God.

But the Holy Spirit produces this kind of fruit in our lives: love, joy, peace, patience, kindness, goodness, faithfulness, gentleness, and self-control. There is no law against these things! (5)

People try many different things to take money out of the hands of others in an attempt to place it under their own control. For instance, we earn wages, someone pays us their money, and then we purchase things we need, giving up portions of our money willingly. Some salesmen can be very effective at getting folks to part with some of their money for things they don't need. Sometimes we spend money on things we simply want, whether we need them or not. We see money exchanged everyday for a multitude of reasons. Often the intent is neither good nor bad.

Those desiring to live godly lives in Christ Jesus should always be careful to guard their heart and watch their motivations with the handling of money. Those motivations are equally important to the giving and the receiving of money. We do not need to use the practices of the world, or as stated earlier, the flesh to acquire or manipulate others with the use of money.

ROBBING GOD | 55

In Matthew 21:12 and 13, Jesus turned the money tables over, because men had turned God's house into a *"den of thieves."* (6) Jesus always knew the real thoughts and intents of men's hearts, and he also knew those money changers were more interested in making a profit at the expense of the penitent than they were in the atonement sought at the temple.

There are many practices used today that could get a few people thrown out of the *temple* if Jesus were around. Jesus did not use gimmicks to get people to support his ministry. He didn't offer engraved name tags in exchange for large donations to purchase new jets to carry the gospel around the world. He didn't tell the crowds gathered around him that all they had to do to be blessed and financially prosperous was to send him a thousand dollars.

Neither do I recall Jesus teaching his disciples that they could receive a hundredfold blessing and receive tons of money if they would faithfully sow a seed of a hundred, a thousand, or even ten thousand dollars into his ministry. We are inundated with offers from the left and the right, from the right and the wrong, from the saints and the shysters, as well as the sinners and the salesmen who are banking on our desire to get something for nothing.

Unfortunately, it's really not *just* about them and the techniques they use to get us to give up our money. It's about our hearts and our reasons for giving money to them. It's about our motivations and expectations, and the price we are willing to pay in order to prosper. It's about our willingness to risk what we've earned by throwing it out in hopes of getting a tremendous blessing, rather than being tremendously blessed by working hard and prospering according to our efforts. Why would we work hard to be blessed if we believed everything could be given to us in great quantities only by sowing a little?

The sad thing is the only people getting rich by most of the giving methods we discussed earlier are the casinos, the lottery commissions, and the preachers to whom everyone is giving their money. Notice I said *giving* to them. They aren't taking any of it from us. They have learned to benefit from our hopes and willingness to think we can get money for nothing—so they stand there willingly receiving the offerings we so desperately present to the *god of money* in hope of receiving a hundredfold blessing.

What are the basic realities about receiving wages? God worked! Look at the account of creation in Genesis, and you will see that God not only worked at creation, but he also rested when he finished. Adam also worked! God created the garden and put Adam in it to take care of its needs. When Adam fell, God did not curse *work* anymore than he cursed *childbirth*. God told Adam the ground would be cursed, that his work would be harder, and that Eve's childbirth would now be painful. In Genesis 5:28 and 29, when Noah was born, his father Lamech prayed thus:

May he bring us relief from our work and the painful labor of farming this ground that the Lord has cursed. (7)

Adam messed up and God added sweat. *(8)* However, there are still many verses throughout the Bible that tell about work and how it is blessed and rewarded according to our effort and expectation. Even the devil complained to God about how God had blessed Job's work. *(9)* Psalms 62:12 states:

> *Also to You, O Lord, belongs mercy; for you render to each one according to his work. (10)*

We should not think that particular verse is only about the after-life. God blesses and rewards hard work, and we should never be hesitant to perform it. Apparently, the early church also had to address the matter of work, because there were folks in their midst who also wanted something for nothing.

> *Even while we were with you, we gave you this command: "Those unwilling to work will not get to eat." Yet we hear that some of you are living idle lives, refusing to work and meddling in other people's business. We command such people and urge them in the name of the Lord Jesus Christ to settle down and work to earn their own living. (11)*

I say all this for several reasons. One of which is my disdain for hearing people often refer to being blessed as if *not working* is a blessing. I will admit there are many things that I have to work at, that I would like to change. However, it is not the *act of work* that bothers me. I find tremendous fulfillment and excitement in the *work of my hands,* because I know I am doing what God has given me to do...and according to the Scripture, there is nothing better.

> *Wherefore I perceive that there is nothing better, than that a man should rejoice in his own works; for that is his portion: for who shall bring him to see what shall be after him? (12)*

Another one of my reasons involves giving. I am also tired of people giving only for the reason of anticipated personal gain. It makes no difference whether our giving is to the church of the casino, the church of the lottery, or the church of religion—if we only give to get, how are we blessed? I am certainly not against giving. I love to give, and I am sure that I give more than some, and less than others. However, I refuse to give grudgingly, and for selfish motivations, because I have nothing that I did not receive. *(13)* I give cheerfully because I love to give, and I love to obey the word of God.

Therefore, this has all been said to say this: let us put forth great efforts and be filled with tremendous expectation that God will bless us and reward us according to all that we do. Let us do all that we do cheerfully and with all our might; that we might find peace, joy, purpose, fulfillment and contentment in all that God has given us to do. If that is not what we are experiencing, let's seek God to discover what it is that we should be doing in order to experience genuine blessings. We should all experience the enjoyment and prosperity that comes from comprehending and doing what God has set before us to do each day.

> *Work willingly at whatever you do, as though you were working for the Lord rather than for people. Remember that the Lord will give you an inheritance as your reward, and that the Master you are serving is Christ. (14)*

Chapter Eight:

Part 4 of the Parable
"Stressing Sunday"

Sitting in the den, tired and worn out from the day's events, Mom and Dad decided their day had been stressful enough without finishing the evening in a fight over finances. Mom could always tell how stressed-out Dad was about the bills. She tried to keep most of her worrying about money to herself, because she didn't want to stress Dad any more than she knew he was already. She had learned to quietly trust God to take care of the needs of her family, and sometimes she had to remind Dad that God was her source and not him. They didn't know how they could have avoided anything that happened that day so there was no sense playing the blame game, or saying things they would regret later. Mom sat quietly reading a book to relax, and Dad practiced a little more channel surfing before they called it a night.

Sunday morning Dad awoke to the sounds of children running up and down the hallway outside of his bedroom. Mom had gotten up earlier with the baby and was in the kitchen. She had slipped quietly out of the room, leaving him to get some extra sleep.

Once good and awake, Dad grabbed his robe and headed downstairs. The smell of fresh coffee had a hypnotic affect, drawing him to the location of its aroma. Mom greeted him with a morning kiss and handed him the baby.

Dad took a seat at the breakfast table, holding the baby, while Mom got him a cup of coffee. The kids had already finished their breakfast, and Mom told them to go to their rooms to get ready for church. Dad held the baby on one leg as he ate warmed-up pancakes and cold bacon. Mom had gone back upstairs to get ready for church, and Dad stayed behind cleaning the kitchen while still holding the baby.

They still had plenty of time before having to leave for church, so Dad took the baby and went into the den. Dad placed the baby in the playpen and kicked back in his favorite chair to finish another cup of coffee. Grabbing the remote, he turned on the television and began flipping channels for something to watch.

Sunday morning television was full of the usual morning commentary and news programs. Dad was worn out with the over-worked subject of politics. With the economic turmoil at full steam, the news reporters were having a feeding frenzy trying to decide who to blame for all the money woes. It was too early for Dad to stomach their barrage of commentary, so he moved on to other channels. Some of the local churches had programs to watch on Sunday morning. Then of course, there were the nationally televised programs by the big TV preachers. Those were the guys who wore Dad out more than politics and reality shows combined. Mainly because they preached ten-minute sermons and then used every reason in the world to beg for money during the other twenty minutes of their thirty minute broadcast.

There was one guy, however, that Dad watched occasionally. He really liked his preaching. That TV preacher always had something very simple and encouraging to say. Dad was amazed whenever he caught the guy's program, because he had never seen him pull for an offering on the broadcast. Offerings were a sore spot for Dad. Not because he was stingy, but because some TV preachers acted so greedy, in Dad's opinion, and begged for money so often. He watched a lot more Christian television years ago. He was hungry for God's word, and it excited him to be able to hear the word of God from different sources without having to rely on one sermon on Sunday morning to keep him going through the week. He had noticed, however, that over the recent years, less of the word got preached, and begging and selling seemed to rule the day.

The last straw for Dad happened a little over a year ago. He watched a well-known preacher spend fifteen minutes giving an intense sermon on faith and prosperity. Then he was amazed when the same guy spent the last fifteen minutes of the broadcast saying they would have to take their ministry program off the air if everyone watching his show failed to send in one hundred dollars or more. The preacher promised that everyone would get a hundredfold blessing for sending a *seed faith offering* to him immediately. Wow, that's quite a promise, thought Dad. Send him a hundred dollars and wait for God to return ten thousand dollars.

It occurred to Dad, while watching this guy, that if it really worked that way, then God would give everyone ten thousand dollars who sent this preacher one hundred dollars. If the preacher believed his own preaching, maybe he should consider practicing what he preached, and send everyone on his mailing list one hundred dollars so God could bless him with enough money to keep his program on the air. Dad felt really uncomfortable thinking that way about some of the preachers he saw on television. He didn't want to judge them falsely, but he could never shake the feeling that something was wrong with a lot of that type of preaching regarding money. At any rate, he wasn't sure who to talk to about the subject for fear of being accused of wrongly judging a minister.

Mom walked into the den and interrupted Dad's thoughts by suggesting he go get ready for church. She took the baby from the playpen, and Dad jumped up from his chair and headed upstairs. It never took him long to get ready. He could pull it off in twenty minutes, and someone else in the house would still need some last minute prodding to get to church on time.

Soon the family was filing out of the front door of the house and climbing in the van to make the short drive to church. Dad went throughout the house turning off lights and checking doors and windows. He ran to the den and grabbed his checkbook before setting the alarm, and locked the dead-bolt on the front door. He never got back to his budget situation after the emergency room and the extra takeout meal. He knew he would be putting something in the offering plate, so he had the checkbook in order to be prepared.

He was familiar with what the preacher always suggested for him to put in the offering, but he wasn't sure what he could spare for the week. Ten percent of the family's income was easy math, but giving it up every week without question had proven to be a task that drained their budget and their joy. Dad, more than anything, wished giving hadn't become such a frustrating process, because it distracted him from much needed and appreciated edification at church. Dad was no theologian, but he did read his Bible often. Sometimes he hated the way he doubted what he heard some preachers say on different subjects—especially giving. But the way some of those guys used Bible verses to promote *their* budgets and *their* agendas left Dad wondering if they were reading the same Bible he read.

Chapter Nine:

Part 5 of the Parable "*The Sunday Offering*"

The family finally made it to church for another Sunday morning. They always arrived out of breath and in a rush, looking for a parking space, herding the kids into the building, escorting kids to Children's Church, and taking the baby to the nursery. It's a miracle they managed to survive the family trip to the service. Dad has always wondered how anyone could relax long enough to get anything out of a church service after the kind of intense workout they went through just to make it to the pew.

By the time Mom and Dad entered the sanctuary and found a place to sit, the worship team was already leading the congregation in singing, and Dad was ready for a break. It was hard for him to jump into the spirit of things after the morning wrestling match with time constraints and children. Mom sang along. She had the ability to adjust to daily changes and interruptions that Dad seemed to lack. They tended to balance each other out in a lot of ways. That was one of the main reasons their relationship worked so well.

Dad was still distracted by his intercepted and incomplete budget struggle. He was always ready and willing to give money to the church, but he wasn't comfortable with an amount he could afford to give today. He also hated feeling guilty and pressured every time the offering was taken. He wanted to blame the church for his stress, but he did realize he put most of it on himself. It seemed he was always being reminded of the church's need for more money, but the church to him, never seemed to demonstrate concern about his need for more money. Dad was tired of his heart sickening and mentally distracting battle over money. He just wanted to be at peace.

Soon the song service came to an end, and everyone took their seats. Dad had the drill memorized—song service, special music, announcements, offering, preaching, and altar call. The Sunday morning service had become a predictable experience. Some mornings, even a crying baby was a welcomed distraction just to break the monotony. He slipped his checkbook out of his jacket pocket and began making out a check. He decided to leave the amount blank until the last minute, because he still wasn't sure what he could afford to give. Dad knew he still had a little time to decide while the special music and the announcements were going on before the offering.

Suddenly, Dad was surprised to hear his pastor's voice addressing the congregation. That was unusual. The pastor always started after the offering. Unless of course, he was making one of his pitches for more money for some special need or reason.ABad's guard went up like the cat's ears go back when being bothered by one of the kids. Not this week, thought Dad; he was already having a particularly rough time with the whole giving issue.

Dad looked up from his checkbook and took a close look at the pastor. The pastor didn't seem to be himself this morning. Something was different. Dad's attention piqued as he heard the pastor say he wanted to do something different that morning. The pastor said he wanted to share honestly from his heart about some issues that God had been dealing with him about.

Dad listened carefully as he heard his pastor ask the congregation to take a deep breath and relax. The pastor continued to tell the congregation not to worry about the special music, or the announcements, or even the offering, because he had something really important to discuss with them.

Dad scratched his right ear and wondered if he had just heard what he thought he heard. Did his pastor just say not to worry about the offering? Even Dad was paying attention now. He never dreamed he would ever hear a preacher say not to worry about the offering. Everyone worried about the offering. Their church didn't have anything to sell like other businesses. The whole church budget revolved around everyone's giving.

The preacher was softer spoken and appeared a little broken-hearted as he shared. He didn't seem to be following his notes very closely and spoke as though he was talking one-on-one with each one of the folks in the pews. Dad was really touched by the pastor's demeanor and let his guard down somewhat to actually hear what the pastor had to say.

The pastor opened his Bible and read from the book of Ephesians:

> *So now you Gentiles are no longer strangers and foreigners. You are citizens along with all of God's holy people. You are members of God's family. Together, we are his house, built on the foundation of the apostles and the prophets. And the cornerstone is Christ Jesus himself. We are carefully joined together in him, becoming a holy temple for the Lord. (15)*

Closing his Bible and humbly looking across the room at his congregation, the pastor began to share from his heart about those verses. He said, "I have to confess to you, my dear church, that God has been dealing with me and revealing to me that I have been viewing his church, his body, in some ways that need correcting. Many times I have stood in this pulpit and told you all what God's word declares about how you should live. Today, I want to tell you some things that the word says about me and how I should live as your pastor.

"First of all, we are citizens together, we are family together, we are all together his house. I no longer want to use the pulpit as a device that I can hide behind or keep myself separated from you. Many of the things you struggle with, I battle with as well. I don't want you to be afraid to be open with me about your struggles. I don't want to be afraid to be vulnerable with you about my own battles. If we truly are citizens and family in the same house, then our house needs to be a house of trust. It should be a safe-house for each of us. I am not a probation officer that you have to report to each week so you can stay out of hell. I am your brother in Christ, and I need you as much as I need to be needed by you."

By that time church didn't feel the same. The service had turned into something much different. Dad could hear quiet weeping from some of the people in the congregation. He even noticed Mom's eyes tearing up; that almost made him lose it. He knew his pastor was a good guy, but now Dad was deciding he *really* liked the man. Dad was always more appreciative of painful honesty over insincere and phony joy. He began to pray under his breath for his pastor. He wanted him to be able to complete what he had set out to do that morning.

The pastor bravely and broken-heartedly continued, "Secondly, God's church is built on the foundation of the teachings of the apostles and the prophets, with Christ being the chief cornerstone. I also must confess to you that I have not performed my office correctly. I have worked and done my job according to many of my own thoughts and desires as if the church was built on my foundation. That is not what the word declares, and it is probably the reason why much of what we do doesn't work for you or those of us in leadership.

"You see," he let out a nervous chuckle, "often, I am as bored with what we do in our services as you are. There, I have now admitted it, and you may also. If God has joined us together to become a holy temple in him, then we must start with a new and fresh level of honesty and openness. We need to become a holy people together. I cannot make you holy with my preaching or my skills, nor is it my responsibility. We must function as a body and be the church together on God's terms, or it is no longer acceptable to me. I fear the day has come that it is no longer acceptable to God."

Dad was now one of those quietly crying congregants. He loved God, and he loved the church, but he always felt that many things within the structure had gone the wrong direction. He longed to be a part of a local congregation that was more interested in God's way than their own way or perception. Could this awakening actually be happening to Dad's church? He hoped so!

Then the pastor went on to say, "Contrary to popular thinking, I do not possess all the gifts necessary to make this local church function as an expression of the Body of Christ. I only have the gifts and the talents that God has given to me. When I attempt to do all the thinking and all the work for this body, we all suffer and lack, because I honestly can't do all that we need to become a healthy church. God has placed many talents and gifts in this church, and I need them as much as you need them. Not only that, you need to be using the gifts you possess in this local assembly instead of burying them in yourselves!

"Read with me in Romans, Chapter 12, verses 4 through 18. Now be patient. I realize these are a lot of verses, but it is very important that we understand these things together."

The whole congregation must have opened their Bibles and looked for Romans, Chapter 12. Dad hadn't heard that much ruffling paper and page turning in his church for a long time. He could still hear some crying and nose-blowing. He was amazed at the number of people wiping their eyes periodically as the service continued. The pastor was wiping his eyes, too.

"Is everyone at Romans, Chapter twelve?" inquired the pastor. "Okay, follow with me:

> *Just as our bodies have many parts and each part has a special function, so it is with Christ's body. We are many parts of one body, and we all belong to each other. In his grace, God has*

given us different gifts for doing certain things well.

So if God has given you the ability to prophesy, speak out with as much faith as God has given you. If your gift is serving others, serve them well. If you are a teacher, teach well. If your gift is to encourage others, be encouraging. If it is giving, give generously. If God has given you leadership ability, take the responsibility seriously. And if you have a gift for showing kindness to others, do it gladly.

Don't just pretend to love others. Really love them. Hate what is wrong. Hold tightly to what is good. Love each other with genuine affection, and take delight in honoring each other. Never be lazy, but work hard and serve the Lord enthusiastically. Rejoice in our confident hope. Be patient in trouble, and keep on praying. When God's people are in need, be ready to help them. Always be eager to practice hospitality.

Bless those who persecute you. Don't curse them; pray that God will bless them. Be happy with those who are happy, and weep with those who weep. Live in harmony with each other. Don't be too proud to enjoy the company of ordinary people. And don't think you know it all!

Never pay back evil with more evil. Do things in such a way that everyone can see you *are honorable. Do all that you can to live in peace with everyone. (16)*

"The verses in this chapter reveal some of the many ways God instructs us on how to become a good local church body. I know that I am gifted to do some of these tasks. I believe some of you could do them better than me. I have seen the generosity and the kindness that you have shown to my family. I can only assume that you also use and share those same gifts with each other. If I am wrong in that assumption, please begin today using what God has given you to help others within this church and beyond these walls.

"I recognize that some of you are very gifted preachers and teachers. This body needs your gift! Help me learn how to make room for your gift in God's church so we can all learn and be edified.

"I acknowledge that God has planted great leaders within this congregation. I apologize for not utilizing your abilities. I repent, and I promise that I will learn to rely on and benefit from the talents God has given you. I will refrain from fear and insecurity and will learn to trust God and the leaders he has placed in this fellowship to help us all grow into a healthier and stronger church.

"Now to those of you that have the gift of encouraging others, please use your gift freely. Encourage us to notice the good things God is doing among his body. Help us to use that recognition to be less critical. Show us a more positive way to live together in peace. Equip us with a joyful outlook on what we have in Christ, so we can become a more attractive expression of God's Church to the world in which we live."

The pastor stopped speaking for a moment and took his handkerchief out of his pocket and wiped his eyes and his nose. The sounds of soft weeping, sniffling noses, throat-clearing, and coughing continued as the pastor paused.

Then the pastor cleared his throat and continued speaking to the congregation. They had managed to move beyond stunned disbelief and were now entering a level of repentance and brokenness which had not been felt here in some time. Dad had stopped feeling his own pain and was now empathizing with his pastor. He knew how difficult this had to be for him. Dad realized this was not an overnight revelation for the pastor. He admired the courage it took for his pastor to do what he was doing.

"Now, let's talk about money. I am aware that most of you are worn out with the subject. Trust me. I am worn out and disgusted with bringing it up to you all the time. I have decided to conduct an experiment. The verses we read mentioned the gift of giving. I have noticed throughout my years of pastoring in various churches that there were always a few people in each congregation that had the ability to give much more than many of the rest of the members. I have come to believe that those individuals had a *gift of giving*, and that God places individuals like that in local bodies for his purpose and for the benefit of his church.

"I want to encourage those among you that believe your gift is giving, to do as the scriptures say, and give generously. Through your wise and generous sowing, you have reaped a bountiful harvest, and God has gifted you with the ability to provide a generous portion of the needs of his local body. For that, we thank you very much. For the rest of you that give out of your abundance, or as the widow in the Bible that gave all she had, I ask you to simply give what you are capable of giving cheerfully.

"God's kingdom is not the stock market, and it is obvious by what we have seen in the news that we have to trust God, because trusting in the financial markets of men can be disappointing and devastating. Your giving is not meant to be used as a tool for your personal gain, alone. It is an expression of love, regardless of the percentage of your income you choose to give. If one hundred percent of it is not given cheerfully, then I no longer want it in our offering plates. If my experiment fails, then I will be glad to join the ranks of great men of God, like Paul, and go work with my hands while continuing to joyfully be your pastor."

Dad closed his checkbook and put it back into his coat pocket. He realized the pastor had obviously checked his own heart about giving, and now it was time for Dad to check his heart.

The pastor wasn't finished. He turned in his Bible to Matthew 23:23, and began to read to the congregation:

> *"You're hopeless, you religion scholars and Pharisees! Frauds! You keep meticulous*

account books, tithing on every nickel and dime you get, but on the meat of God's Law, things like fairness and compassion and commitment—the absolute basics!—you carelessly take it or leave it. Careful bookkeeping is commendable, but the basics are required." (17)

"Church, in this verse, Jesus is speaking to the men in my profession. I confess and repent. I have not been called by God to be your bookkeeper. I am your pastor. That is my call and my gift. It takes more than what I have, and have been called to be, to make a church. From this day forward we will do as Jesus said, and we will pay attention to the very important basics.

"Furthermore, I am aware that many of you enjoy watching Christian television shows, and there are plenty of preachers on TV for you to choose from. Many of the shows appear to be nothing more than infomercials with something to sell. There are a few national and local ministers that don't spend all their air time pleading for money. I appreciate the fact that there are more sources than me and our church for spiritual food. Believe me; I don't eat in the same restaurant every time I go out.

"Nevertheless, as your pastor I offer this for you to consider. Some of those programs insist you make *seed faith contributions* to their ministries with promises of great financial reward and payback. Please consider another example in the Scriptures:

"When one of you says, I am a follower of Paul, and another says, I follow Apollos, aren't you acting just like people of the world? After all, who is Apollos? Who is Paul? We are only God's servants through whom you believed the Good News. Each of us did the work the Lord gave us. I planted the seed in your hearts, and Apollos watered it, but it was God who made it grow. It's not important who does the planting, or who does the watering. What's important is that God makes the seed grow. The one who plants and the one who waters work together with the same purpose. And both will be rewarded for their own hard work. For we are both God's workers. And you are God's field. You are God's building." (18)

"Church, remember this, God makes your seed grow. My encouragement to you is this, plant generously and sow cheerfully into your own field, and trust God to make it grow. As the scriptures say:

For God is the one who provides seed for the farmer and then bread to eat. In the same way, he will provide and increase your resources and then produce a great harvest of generosity in you. (19)

The pastor paused briefly and collected himself, and with a quiet and broken heart completed his morning message with these comments. "My friends and my family, just as we read together, it is my utmost desire that we as a body, belonging to Christ, learn to live in peace with all men and with ourselves.

"I know you weren't expecting this when you came to service today. Neither was I. I hope that I haven't scared you or offended you by my words or my demeanor. I no longer intend to proceed with my life by blindly practicing the religious traditions that have been handed down to me unless they are grounded and established in God's word. I am hungry to be the best man I can be in Christ, and I desire this to be the best local expression of his body that we can become, together. Relax, God isn't finished. But, he is able to finish that good work he has begun in us. I love you all, and I consider it an honor to be your pastor. I can no longer do this alone. I need your help to finish the task set before us."

The people were so engrossed in the pastor's words that it took a minute for them to realize he was finished. His message had inspired freedom in their spirits and hope in their minds.

Dad had never been in a service like this. People began to stand to their feet and applaud the pastor. Soon, everyone was standing and applauding. The wave of freedom surging from his words and from God's Spirit washed over the entire congregation. The people felt an enormous outpouring of love for God, for their pastor, and for each other.

Dad knew the place wasn't going to be the same. He knew he would never be the same. That was it. The service ended. No special music, no announcements, and no offering. Nevertheless, Dad took his checkbook out of his pocket, opened it to the partially written check, and filled in a generous amount—cheerfully. He placed it on a table at the back of the sanctuary where many other cheerful offerings had been placed. His heart was so touched to see the amount of giving that had taken place when an offering hadn't even been requested.

As Dad gathered his family and headed to the van, he thought about how glad he was that he hadn't played hooky this particular Sunday morning. He also realized, if he had missed such a special moment, he would probably still be struggling with an attitude he was long over-due to give up. Dad remembered just how grateful he was to be a part of God's church, the Body of Christ.

The Summation

Is it really possible to *rob God*? If so, who is capable of *robbing God*? For many years I have watched offerings taken up in many places and in many ways. I've heard and witnessed the simple, the sublime, and the ridiculous. It is not difficult for us to understand giving. There is something within all of us, a part of our nature that wants to give. Our hearts respond to the needs of others. We see ordinary heroes jump into action everyday when people are in trouble. Giving is as natural for us as receiving. If we made a list of all the ways we give on a daily basis, we would truly be amazed. Opening a door, helping a child, picking up the tab for lunch, sharing a cookie, saying a prayer, offering an encouraging word—there is really no end to the list. We do it willingly and without coercion or manipulation the majority of the time.

All of us are givers. Giving is not just a rich man's game. Jesus called attention to a poor elderly widow woman that with two pennies gave more than all he witnessed giving at a temple. He also informed us that by giving to the least we were also giving to him. How is it that we have managed to take the joy out of so much of our giving? When did we succumb to thinking that the only good giving involved giving to us? When did it become about us? When did it become about money? I can't accept that God's love for a cheerful giver is limited to cash. God gave his son. Jesus gave his life. What little we give should at the very least be given cheerfully.

What does it take to be a giver? Being a giver is not contingent on what one has to give. Not only is it natural for all to give, we all have *something* to give. Not only did the lazy servant fail to recognize what the good master had given him, he failed to understand that he had to give in order to profit. Profit comes from putting something at risk and watching it pay off. With or without cash, we have plenty to offer, or to put at risk. That's what happens when we give. We are making ourselves vulnerable to those we give to. Not everyone appreciates our help or our giving, even when it is given freely. That is certainly obvious from the fact that there are many who fail to appreciate or even believe that God gave them anything.

The crux of the matter for this little book is that it is not written to coerce us to give, nor is it intended to get us to stop giving. It is offered to help us recapture the sheer joy of giving. Remember, God loves a cheerful giver. Giving under duress, manipulation, and guilt quite simply takes all the fun out of giving. We cannot be cheerful under those circumstances. Jesus endured the cross and the cost of *giving* because of the *joy (20)* that awaited him. We need to check our hearts and evaluate our motives for giving. We also need to reconsider the way we tolerate some forms of solicitations for giving within our lives and our churches. In other words, when we watch people take up offerings in our churches or on TV using techniques that make us uncomfortable—methods that we believe to be wrong or unscriptural, we should confront it openly and honestly.

When I first received the inspiration to write this book, it came with this thought, *"The axe needs to be laid to the root of the money tree within the church, because it is grieving the Holy Spirit."* Let's go back to look at the time Jesus commented about the woman who put two pennies in the offering in Mark 12:41-44.

> *Jesus sat down near the collection box in the Temple and watched as the crowds dropped in their money. Many rich people put in large amounts. Then a poor widow came and dropped in two small coins.*
>
> *Jesus called his disciples to him and said, "I tell you the truth, this poor widow has given more than all the others who are making contributions. For they gave a tiny part of their*

surplus, but she, poor as she is, has given everything she had to live on." (21)

Imagine what would happen if Jesus walked into one of our churches and sat next to the offering plate and watched what everyone put in it. We would probably ask him to leave or escort him out of the building. Yet, we tolerate people in our midst who use every trick in the book to collect money, and we think nothing of it—or we say nothing even though we are thinking it. I am not interested in joining the theological debate on tithing. The government takes more than 10% from us. If our giving to God is limited to a cash settlement of 10%, have we found the joy in giving? If giving is a like a tax or an obligation, can we really give cheerfully? I think we all know that answer. God loves a cheerful giver. I can't come up with a better way to describe a more enjoyable way to give, than cheerfully.

So here it is, I pray we have an *"aha!"* moment like the Dad in our story—a moment to let our guard down to experience the joy of giving—a moment to learn how to recognize and resist the guilt-driven, coerced, and manipulated giving that robs us of the joy of giving.

The next time you hear someone quoting the book of Malachi when taking up an offering, especially the part about *robbing God,* go read Malachi in its entirety. It only contains four short chapters. You will discover that Malachi's message about *robbing God* was directed to the priests of his time. It is scripturally and contextually inaccurate for clergy to use Malachi's words as a whip to emotionally manipulate an offering out of the faithful by suggesting they are *robbing God* if they don't give to them. When they act in this manner to solicit money, they make themselves guilty of the very behavior God directed Malachi to address. If we trust God and trust one another, we need not, out of fear, rely on manipulative practices to fund God's work. A cheerful God provides for his children, and he loves it when we cheerfully give.

Appendix

Chronological list of Scriptures

1)   Matthew 25:14-30

14. "Again, the Kingdom of Heaven can be illustrated by the story of a man going on a long trip. He called together his servants and entrusted his money to them while he was gone.

15. He gave five bags of silver to one, two bags of silver to another, and one bag of silver to the last—dividing it in proportion to their abilities. He then left on his trip.

16. "The servant who received the five bags of silver began to invest the money and earned five more.

17. The servant with two bags of silver also went to work and earned two more.

18. But the servant who received the one bag of silver dug a hole in the ground and hid the master's money.

19. "After a long time their master returned from his trip and called them to give an account of how they had used his money.

20. The servant to whom he had entrusted the five bags of silver came forward with five more and said, 'Master, you gave me five bags of silver to invest, and I have earned five more.'

21. "The master was full of praise. 'Well done, my good and faithful servant. You have been faithful in handling this small amount, so now I will give you many more responsibilities. Let's celebrate together!'

22. "The servant who had received the two bags of silver came forward and said, 'Master, you gave me two bags of silver to invest, and I have earned two more.'

23. "The master said, 'Well done, my good and faithful servant. You have been faithful in handling this small amount, so now I will give you many more responsibilities. Let's celebrate together!'

24. "Then the servant with the one bag of silver came and said, 'Master, I knew you were a harsh man, harvesting crops you didn't plant and gathering crops you didn't cultivate.

25. I was afraid I would lose your money, so I hid it in the earth. Look, here is your money back.'

26. "But the master replied, 'You wicked and lazy servant! If you knew I harvested crops I didn't plant and gathered crops I didn't cultivate,

27. why didn't you deposit my money in the bank? At least I could have gotten some interest on it.'

28. "Then he ordered, 'Take the money from this servant, and give it to the one with the ten bags of silver.

29. To those who use well what they are given, even more will be given, and they will have an abundance. But from those who do nothing, even what little they have will be taken away.

30. Now throw this useless servant into outer darkness, where there will be weeping and gnashing of teeth.'
Holy Bible, New Living Translation ®, copyright © 1996, 2004 by Tyndale Charitable Trust. Used by permission of Tyndale House Publishers. All rights reserved.

2) Romans 1:16-17

16. For I am not ashamed of the gospel of Christ, for it is the power of God to salvation for everyone who believes, for the Jew first and also for the Greek.

17. For in it the righteousness of God is revealed from faith to faith; as it is written, "The just shall live by faith."
NKJV

3) 2 Corinthians 9:6-15

6. Remember this—a farmer who plants only a few seeds will get a small crop. But the one who plants generously will get a generous crop.

7. You must each decide in your heart how much to give. And don't give reluctantly or in response to pressure. "For God loves a person who gives cheerfully."

8. And God will generously provide all you need. Then you will always have everything you need and plenty left over to share with others.

9. As the Scriptures say, "They share freely and give generously to the poor. Their good deeds will be remembered forever."

10. For God is the one who provides seed for the farmer and then bread to eat. In the same way, he will provide and increase your resources and then produce a great harvest of generosity in you.

11. Yes, you will be enriched in every way so that you can always be generous. And when we take your gifts to those who need them, they will thank God.

12. So two good things will result from this ministry of giving—the needs of the believers in Jerusalem will be met, and they will joyfully express their thanks to God.

13. As a result of your ministry, they will give glory to God. For your generosity to them and to all believers will prove that you are obedient to the Good News of Christ.

14. And they will pray for you with deep affection because of the overflowing grace God has given to you.

15. Thank God for this gift too wonderful for words!

Holy Bible, New Living Translation ®, copyright © 1996, 2004 by Tyndale Charitable Trust. Used by permission of Tyndale House Publishers. All rights reserved.

4) 1 Timothy 6:10

10. For the love of money is the root of all evil: which while some coveted after, they have erred from the faith, and pierced themselves through with many sorrows.
KJV

5) Galatians 5:19-23

19. When you follow the desires of your sinful nature, the results are very clear: sexual immorality, impurity, lustful pleasures,

20. idolatry, sorcery, hostility, quarreling, jealousy, outbursts of anger, selfish ambition, dissension, division,

21. envy, drunkenness, wild parties, and other sins like these. Let me tell you again, as I have before, that anyone living that sort of life will not inherit the Kingdom of God.

22. But the Holy Spirit produces this kind of fruit in our lives: love, joy, peace, patience, kindness, goodness, faithfulness,

23. gentleness, and self-control. There is no law against these things!

Holy Bible, New Living Translation ®, copyright © 1996, 2004 by Tyndale Charitable Trust. Used by permission of Tyndale House Publishers. All rights reserved.

ROBBING GOD | 93

6) Matthew 21:12-13

12. Then Jesus went into the temple of God and drove out all those who bought and sold in the temple, and overturned the tables of the money changers and the seats of those who sold doves.

13. And He said to them, "It is written, 'My house shall be called a house of prayer,' but you have made it a 'den of thieves.'"
NKJV

7) Genesis 5:28-29

28. Lamech lived one hundred and eighty-two years, and had a son.

29. And he called his name Noah, saying, "This one will comfort us concerning our work and the toil of our hands, because of the ground which the Lord has cursed."
NKJV

8) Genesis 3:19

19. In the sweat of your face you shall eat bread 'till you return to the ground, for out of it you were taken; for dust you are, and to dust you shall return."
NKJV

9) Job 1:10

10. Have You not made a hedge around him, around his household, and around all that he has on every side? You have blessed the work of his hands, and his possessions have increased in the land.
NKJV

10) Psalms 62:12

12. Also to You, O Lord, belongs mercy; For You render to each one according to his work.
NKJV

11) 2 Thessalonians 3:10-12

10. Even while we were with you, we gave you this command: "Those unwilling to work will not get to eat."

11. Yet we hear that some of you are living idle lives, refusing to work and meddling in other people's business.

12. We command such people and urge them in the name of the Lord Jesus Christ to settle down and work to earn their own living.
Holy Bible, New Living Translation ®, copyright © 1996, 2004 by Tyndale Charitable Trust. Used by permission of Tyndale House Publishers. All rights reserved.

12) Ecclesiastes 3:22

22. Wherefore I perceive that there is nothing better, than that a man should rejoice in his own works; for that is his portion: for who shall bring him to see what shall be after him?
KJV

13) 1 Corinthians 4:7

7. For who makes you differ from another? And what do you have that you did not receive? Now if you did indeed receive it, why do you boast as if you had not received it?
NKJV

14) Colossians 3:23-24

23. Work willingly at whatever you do, as though you were working for the Lord rather than for people.

24. Remember that the Lord will give you an inheritance as your reward, and that the Master you are serving is Christ.
Holy Bible, New Living Translation ®, copyright © 1996, 2004 by Tyndale Charitable Trust. Used by permission of Tyndale House Publishers. All rights reserved.

15) Ephesians 2:19-21

19. So now you Gentiles are no longer strangers and foreigners. You are citizens along with all of God's holy people. You are members of God's family.
20. Together, we are his house, built on the foundation of the apostles and the prophets. And the cornerstone is Christ Jesus himself.
21. We are carefully joined together in him, becoming a holy temple for the Lord.

Holy Bible, New Living Translation ®, copyright © 1996, 2004 by Tyndale Charitable Trust. Used by permission of Tyndale House Publishers. All rights reserved.

16) Romans 12:4-18

4. Just as our bodies have many parts and each part has a special function,
5. so it is with Christ's body. We are many parts of one body, and we all belong to each other.
6. In his grace, God has given us different gifts for doing certain things well. So if God has given you the ability to prophesy, speak out with as much faith as God has given you.
7. If your gift is serving others, serve them well. If you are a teacher, teach well.
8. If your gift is to encourage others, be encouraging. If it is giving, give generously. If God has given you leadership ability, take the responsibility seriously. And if you have a gift for showing kindness to others, do it gladly.
9. Don't just pretend to love others. Really love them. Hate what is wrong. Hold tightly to what is good.
10. Love each other with genuine affection, and take delight in honoring each other.
11. Never be lazy, but work hard and serve the Lord enthusiastically.
12. Rejoice in our confident hope. Be patient in trouble, and keep on praying.

13. When God's people are in need, be ready to help them. Always be eager to practice hospitality.

14. Bless those who persecute you. Don't curse them; pray that God will bless them.

15. Be happy with those who are happy, and weep with those who weep.

16. Live in harmony with each other. Don't be too proud to enjoy the company of ordinary people. And don't think you know it all!

17. Never pay back evil with more evil. Do things in such a way that everyone can see you are honorable.

18. Do all that you can to live in peace with everyone.

Holy Bible, New Living Translation ®, copyright © 1996, 2004 by Tyndale Charitable Trust. Used by permission of Tyndale House Publishers. All rights reserved.

17)   Matthew 23:23-24

"You're hopeless, you religion scholars and Pharisees! Frauds! You keep meticulous account books, tithing on every nickel and dime you get, but on the meat of God's Law, things like fairness and compassion and commitment — the absolute basics! — you carelessly take it or leave it. Careful bookkeeping is commendable, but the basics are required.
(from THE MESSAGE: The Bible in Contemporary Language © 2002 by Eugene H. Peterson. All rights reserved.)

18)   1 Corinthians 3:4-9

4. When one of you says, "I am a follower of Paul," and another says, "I follow Apollos," aren't you acting just like people of the world?

5. After all, who is Apollos? Who is Paul? We are only God's servants through whom you believed the Good News. Each of us did the work the Lord gave us.

6. I planted the seed in your hearts, and Apollos watered it, but it was God who made it grow.

7. It's not important who does the planting, or who does the watering. What's important is that God makes the seed grow.
8. The one who plants and the one who waters work together with the same purpose. And both will be rewarded for their own hard work.
9. For we are both God's workers. And you are God's field. You are God's building.
Holy Bible, New Living Translation ®, copyright © 1996, 2004 by Tyndale Charitable Trust. Used by permission of Tyndale House Publishers. All rights reserved.

19)   2 Corinthians 9:10
10. For God is the one who provides seed for the farmer and then bread to eat. In the same way, he will provide and increase your resources and then produce a great harvest of generosity in you.
Holy Bible, New Living Translation ®, copyright © 1996, 2004 by Tyndale Charitable Trust. Used by permission of Tyndale House Publishers. All rights reserved.

20)   Hebrews 12:1-3
1. Wherefore seeing we also are compassed about with so great a cloud of witnesses, let us lay aside every weight, and the sin which doth so easily beset us, and let us run with patience the race that is set before us,
2. Looking unto Jesus the author and finisher of our faith; who for the joy that was set before him endured the cross, despising the shame, and is set down at the right hand of the throne of God.
3. For consider him that endured such contradiction of sinners against himself, lest ye be wearied and faint in your minds. KJV

21)   Mark 12:41-44
41. Jesus sat down near the collection box in the Temple and watched as the crowds dropped in their money. Many rich people put in large amounts.
42. Then a poor widow came and dropped in two small coins.

43. Jesus called his disciples to him and said, "I tell you the truth, this poor widow has given more than all the others who are making contributions.

44. For they gave a tiny part of their surplus, but she, poor as she is, has given everything she had to live on."

Holy Bible, New Living Translation ®, copyright © 1996, 2004 by Tyndale Charitable Trust. Used by permission of Tyndale House Publishers. All rights reserved.